JEALOUS FOR YOU

"How Embracing God's Exclusive Love Transforms Your Life"

[Exodus 34:14]

Discover the Power of Wholehearted Worship and Deepen Your Relationship with God.

Shola Ajibade

Jealous For You

Copyrights © 2025

Shola Ajibade

The message in this book reflects the theme of God's passionate love and His call for His people.

Dedication

'In loving memory of my Father
Festus Olusope Omoniyi
You are forever in my heart.'

Shola Ajibade

Acknowledgment

First and foremost, I give all glory and honour to God, the author and finisher of my faith, for His unwavering love, guidance, and grace throughout this journey. Without Him, this book would not have been possible.

In loving memory of my late father, Mr Festus Olusope Omoniyi, whose wisdom and strength continue to inspire me. To my mother, Aduke Omoniyi, your love and resilience have been a constant source of encouragement. Thank you, Mummy.

To my husband, thank you for your unwavering support, patience, and belief in my dreams. I love you, darling. To my wonderful children, you are my pride and joy and the reason I strive to leave a lasting legacy. Mummy loves you always.

To my siblings, thank you for loving and accepting me just as I am. Your support means more to me than words can express.

I am deeply grateful to everyone who believed in me, prayed for me, and encouraged me along the way. Your faith in me has been my strength.

To my amazing family and friends, thank you for standing by me and for your continuous encouragement and love.

To you, the reader of this book, thank you for taking the time to engage with my words, inspired by the Holy Spirit. My hope is that this book blesses and inspires you.

Finally, a heartfelt thank you to the publication and press team for your professionalism and dedication in bringing this book to life.

Table of Contents

Dedication iv
Acknowledgment v
Chapter 1: Introduction to God's Jealousy 1
    Understanding the Concept of Jealousy in Relation to God 1
Chapter 2: The Nature of God's Jealousy 4
    Exploring the Difference Between Human Jealousy and Divine Jealousy 4
        Why God's Jealousy is Rooted in Love? 5
        Practical Reflection: Recognising God's Jealous Love in Your Life . 6
Chapter 3: God's Covenant Relationship 7
    The Importance of Covenant in the Bible 7
    Real-Life Practice: Living in Covenant with God 9
Chapter 4: The Danger Of Idolatry 11
    Defining Idolatry in Modern Times 11
    How Idolatry Impacts Our Relationship with God 12
    Biblical Example: The Rich Young Ruler (Matthew 19:16–22) ... 13
    Real-Life Practice: Identifying and Overcoming Modern Idols ... 13
Chapter 5: Recognising Our Own Idols 15
    Practical Steps to Identify What Competes with God in Our Lives 15
    Ask the Hard Questions 15
    Personal Reflection and Self-Assessment 16
    Breaking Free from Idols 17
    Living with God at the Center 17
Chapter 6: Competing Priorities In Our Heart 19
    Materialism and Wealth 19
    Career and Ambition 19
    Relationships 20
    Social Media and Entertainment 20
    Self-Centeredness 20

- Pride and Reputation 21
- Comfort and Convenience 21
- Success and Achievement 21
- Pleasure and Comfort 22
- Removing Idols and Making God the Centre 22
- Conclusion 23

Chapter 7: God's Call to Holiness 25
- The Call to Live a Life Set Apart for God 25
- Embracing God's Standard for Purity and Devotion 25
- The Transforming Power of Holiness 27
- Real-Life Story: A Life of Holiness Transformed 27
- Conclusion 28

Chapter 8: Exclusive Worship in Modern Times 29
- Understanding the Need for Exclusive Worship in a World Full of Distractions 29
- The Importance of Prioritising God Over Everything Else 30
- Exclusive Worship: A Lifestyle of Devotion 32
- Conclusion 32

Chapter 9: The Role of Prayer and Scripture 34
- How to Develop a Strong Prayer Life and Engage with the Bible . 34
- The Foundation of Prayer Communication with God 34
- Practical Steps to Build a Strong Prayer Life 35
- The Power of Spending Time with God in His Word 35
- Practical Steps for Engaging with Scripture: 36
- Real-Life Example: The Power of Prayer and Scripture in Transformation 37
- Conclusion 37

Chapter 10: Surrendering to God's Will 38
- How to Surrender Every Area of Your Life to God 38
- Steps to Surrender Every Area of Your Life 38
- Letting Go of Control and Trusting in God's Plan 39

Steps to Let Go of Control and Trust God's Plan 40
Real-Life Example: Surrendering to God's Will 41
Conclusion 41

Chapter 11: The Beauty of God's Jealous Love 43
Celebrating the Depth of God's Love That Desires the Best for Us 43
The Joy of Living Fully Devoted to God 44
Real-Life Experience: A Testimony of Devoted 45
Conclusion: The Beauty of God's Jealous Love 46

Chapter 12: Overcoming the Struggle of Divided Loyalties 47
The Challenge of Competing Priorities and How to Overcome Them
.... 47
Practical Strategies for Staying Committed to God 48
Real-Life Example: Navigating Competing Priorities 50
Conclusion: Staying Focused on God 50

Chapter 13: Living in God's Presence 51
Cultivating a Lifestyle That Honours God in All Things 51
Practical Ways to Live in God's Presence 51
The Joy and Peace of Living in God's Presence Every Day 53
Conclusion: Embrace the Beauty of God's Presence 53

Chapter 14: The Rewards of Devotion 55
The Blessings of Wholehearted Devotion to God 55
Biblical Examples of Devotion and Its Rewards 55
God rewards such faith with His faithfulness and provision. 55
Personal Testimonies of Devotion's Rewards 56
The Blessings of Devotion in Modern Life 56
Practical Steps to Deepen Devotion and Experience Its Rewards 57
Conclusion: The Joy of Wholehearted Devotion 58

Chapter 15: A Life Fully Devoted to God 59
Embracing the Call to Exclusive Worship 59
The Transformation of a Devoted Life 59
A Final Invitation to Surrender 60

    Practical Steps to Fully Surrender 60
Chapter 16: Reflection and Prayer.. 62
A Time for Personal Reflection... 62
    Consider the following questions to guide your reflection 62
A Closing Prayer 63
    Let this prayer serve as a guide for surrender and devotion 63
Final Encouragement... 64
Glossary... 65
References 68
Bible References.. 69
Author's Note 73

Chapter 1: Introduction to God's Jealousy

Understanding the Concept of Jealousy in Relation to God

The word jealousy often carries a negative connotation in human relationships, implying insecurity, envy, or mistrust. But in the context of God's character, it is profoundly different. God's jealousy is not born out of weakness or fear but out of His perfect love and holy desire for an exclusive relationship with His people.

In Exodus 34:14, God declares, "Do not worship any other god, for the Lord, whose name is Jealous, is a jealous God." This statement reveals a side of God that may be surprising: His name itself signifies His zeal for our devotion. God's jealousy is rooted in His desire to protect us from anything that could harm or lead us away from Him. It is an expression of His covenantal love—His commitment to us as His people.

Think of it this way: a loving parent is "jealous" because they want what is best for their child. A father wouldn't want his child to trust a stranger with their life, knowing the stranger could harm them. Similarly, God's jealousy is about safeguarding our hearts from idols that can never satisfy us and ensuring that we experience the fullness of His love.

The Significance of God's Desire for Exclusive Worship

God's jealousy is deeply connected to the idea of exclusive worship. In the ancient world, the Israelites were surrounded by cultures that worshipped multiple gods—Baal, Asherah, and others. These idols represented false security and temporary pleasure, but they could not offer the life-giving, eternal relationship that only Yahweh provides.

God's command for exclusive worship is not about His ego; it is about His design for our ultimate good. When we worship anything other than God—money, success, relationships, or even ourselves—we place our trust in something capable of fulfiling us. God desires our whole-hearted devotion because He alone can meet our deepest needs.

Real-life practice can illuminate this truth. Consider a time when you placed your trust in something or someone other than God. Perhaps it was a career you thought would bring you happiness or a relationship you believed would complete you. How did it work out? Many of us find that these pursuits leave us empty, longing for something greater. That longing is a sign of God's jealousy—a gentle reminder that our hearts were made for Him alone.

Practical Application: Cultivating Wholehearted Worship

We must practice wholehearted worship to embrace God's jealousy and deepen our relationship with Him. Here are three steps to consider:

Identify and Remove Idols: Reflect on anything that may have taken God's place in your heart. It might be a habit, a person, or even an attitude. Ask God to reveal these idols and give you the courage to let them go.

Engage in Daily Devotion: Spend time with God through prayer, reading Scripture, and worship. Treat this time as sacred, recognising it as an opportunity to experience His love and guidance.

Surrender Fully: Trust God with every aspect of your life—your relationships, finances, and future. When you surrender to Him, you acknowledge His authority and love, inviting Him to take His rightful place in your heart.

A Transformative Promise: As we understand and embrace God's jealousy, we begin to see it as an invitation to a deeper, more intimate relationship with him. Just as a marriage flourish through exclusive love and unwavering commitment, our relationship with God blossoms when we devote ourselves to worshipping Him alone.

This journey may require sacrifice, but the rewards are eternal. When we embrace God's exclusive love, we experience freedom from the chains of idolatry, the joy of His presence, and the fulfilment of living in alignment with His purpose for our lives.

As we explore this theme further in the coming chapters, may you be encouraged to lean into God's jealous love. He is not a distant deity demanding your obedience but a loving Father who yearns for your heart.

Chapter 2:
The Nature of God's Jealousy

Exploring the Difference Between Human Jealousy and Divine Jealousy

Human jealousy is often fueled by fear, insecurity, and self-interest. It arises when someone feels threatened by the loss of affection, attention, or resources to another. This type of jealousy can be destructive, leading to envy, resentment, or even broken relationships.

Divine jealousy, on the other hand, is wholly pure and rooted in God's unchanging nature. It is an expression of His perfect love, holiness, and righteousness. God's jealousy is not about His needs—He is completely self-sufficient—but about our needs. He knows that only He can provide the fulfilment, security, and peace we desperately seek.

Consider this distinction: human jealousy often seeks to control others for selfish gain, while God's jealousy seeks to protect us for our ultimate good. It is the zeal of a loving Creator who will not allow His children to settle for anything less than the abundant life He has planned for them (John 10:10). His jealousy is not a flaw but a testament to His unwavering commitment to us.

Biblical Examples of God's Jealousy and Why It Is Rooted in Love?

Throughout Scripture, we see examples of God's jealousy in action, always tied to His desire for His people's devotion and well-being.

The Golden Calf Incident (Exodus 32) After delivering the Israelites from slavery in Egypt and entering into a covenant with them, God gave them the Ten Commandments, beginning with, "You shall have no other gods before me" (Exodus 20:3). Yet, while Moses was on Mount Sinai, the people created a golden calf and worshipped it.

God's anger in this situation was not arbitrary but a reflection of His jealousy. He had just demonstrated His power and love through miraculous deliverance, yet His people turned to an idol. His jealousy stemmed from a desire to protect them from the spiritual ruin of idolatry. In response, He disciplined them, not out of spite, but to bring them back to Him.

Hosea and Gomer (Hosea 1–3) The prophet Hosea's relationship with his unfaithful wife, Gomer, is a poignant illustration of God's jealousy. Despite Gomer's repeated infidelity, Hosea is instructed to pursue her and love her, just as God continues to pursue His unfaithful people.

God's jealousy is evident in His longing for His people to return to Him. He is not content to let them drift away into spiritual adultery because He knows that such a path leads to destruction. His jealousy is a demonstration of His relentless love and mercy.

Jesus Cleansing the Temple (John 2:13–17) In the New Testament, Jesus exemplifies God's jealousy when He drives out the money changers from the temple. He declares, "Stop turning my Father's house into a market!" (John 2:16). His actions reveal His zeal for the sanctity of worship and the hearts of those coming to the temple.

Jesus' jealousy was not about the physical building but about the purity of worship. He was passionately protecting the sacredness of the relationship between God and His people.

Why God's Jealousy is Rooted in Love?

At the heart of God's jealousy lies His profound love for us. His jealousy isn't born out of threat or insecurity but from His deep desire for what is best for our lives. His commands to worship Him alone are not restrictive but protective. He knows that worshipping idols—whether they are made of gold, power, or ambition—leads to emptiness and destruction.

Consider the way a parent feels about their child's choices. A parent would be deeply concerned if their child began to trust a harmful friend or engage in self-destructive behaviour. This concern is not about the parent's pride but about their love for the child. In the same way, God's jealousy is His protective love in action.

Practical Reflection: Recognising God's Jealous Love in Your Life

Take a moment to reflect on the times when God may have intervened to draw you back to Him. Perhaps He allowed a relationship to end or a career path to shift, not to harm you but to remove idols that distracted you from Him. These moments, though painful, are evidence of His jealous love working for your good.

Living in Response to God's Jealousy

To live in response to God's jealousy, we must:

Reaffirm Our Allegiance: Regularly examine where our hearts are divided and recommit ourselves to God alone.

Trust His Discipline: Recognise that His correction is a sign of His love and a call to return to Him.

Deepen Our Worship: Cultivate a heart of worship that prioritises God above all else, acknowledging His rightful place in our lives.

As we embrace God's jealousy, we begin to see it not as a limitation but as a profound invitation to experience His unfailing love and unmatched faithfulness. In the next chapter, we will explore the cost of idolatry and how surrendering fully to God brings true freedom and joy.

Chapter 3:
God's Covenant Relationship

The Importance of Covenant in the Bible

The concept of covenant is central to the Bible, serving as the foundation of God's relationship with His people. A covenant is more than a mere contract; it is a sacred bond established by God, rooted in love, faithfulness, and mutual commitment. Unlike human agreements, which can be broken or altered, God's covenants reflect His unchanging nature and His desire for an eternal relationship with us.

From the beginning, God used covenants to reveal His character and redemptive plan. These covenants are not imposed to restrict us but to guide us into the fullness of life He designed. They are marked by promises, responsibilities, and blessings for those who remain faithful.

One of the earliest examples is the covenant with Noah (Genesis 9:8-17), where God promises never to destroy the earth by flood again, signified by the rainbow. Later, God establishes a covenant with Abraham (Genesis 12:1-3; 15:1- 21) to make him the father of many nations and bless all peoples through him. Each covenant builds upon the last, culminating in the New Covenant through Jesus Christ, where believers are reconciled to God through His sacrificial love (Hebrews 8:6-13).

The significance of the covenant lies in its relational nature. It is God saying, "I am yours, and you are Mine." It is His way of drawing us into an exclusive and intimate relationship with Him.

Why God Desires a Faithful and Exclusive Relationship with His People

God's desire for a faithful and exclusive relationship is not born out of selfishness but out of His deep love for us. Faithfulness in this relationship reflects His character, as He is always faithful to His promises. God knows that when our devotion is divided, we are vulnerable to spiritual harm and distance from Him.

In Deuteronomy 7:9, Moses reminds the Israelites, "Know therefore that the Lord your God is God; He is the faithful God, keeping His covenant of love to a thousand generations of those who love Him and keep His commandments." God's faithfulness calls us to respond with exclusive devotion.

Consider the imagery of marriage, frequently used in the Bible to describe God's relationship with His people. In a healthy marriage, faithfulness and exclusivity are essential for trust and intimacy to thrive. Similarly, God calls His people to forsake all other "lovers"—whether they are idols, distractions, or sins—and commit solely to Him. This covenant relationship is not one-sided but requires our willing participation.

Biblical Example: The Sinai Covenant

The covenant made at Mount Sinai is one of the clearest examples of God's desire for an exclusive relationship. In Exodus 19:5-6, God declares, "Now if you obey Me fully and keep My covenant, then out of all nations you will be My treasured possession. Although the whole earth is Mine, you will be for Me a kingdom of priests and a holy nation."

This covenant emphasised the holiness and distinctiveness of God's people. They were called to worship Him alone and live according to His laws, not to earn His love but as a response to the love He had already shown by delivering them from Egypt.

When the Israelites turned to idolatry, worshipping the golden calf, they violated the covenant, breaking God's heart. Yet even then, His faithfulness endured. He renewed the covenant with them, showing that His love is steadfast even when we fall short (Exodus 34:1-10).

Real-Life Practice: Living in Covenant with God

In our modern lives, the concept of covenant can be seen in relationships such as marriage, parenthood, or even close friendships. These relationships thrive on trust, faithfulness, and mutual commitment. When one party breaks that trust, the relationship suffers, but restoration is possible when love and forgiveness prevail.

Consider a marriage where one partner is tempted by outside influences. If they choose to remain faithful, the relationship deepens and flourishes. But if they stray, the bond is damaged. This mirrors our relationship with God. When we allow idols—like materialism, success, or unhealthy relationships—to take priority, we break our covenant with Him. Yet God, in His mercy, always invites us back into fellowship with Him.

In practice, living in covenant with God means:

Daily Commitment: Just as a marriage requires daily acts of love and faithfulness, our relationship with God requires consistent prayer, Scripture reading, and worship.

Repentance and Renewal: When we fall short, we can return to God in repentance, trusting His promise to forgive and restore us (1 John 1:9).

Obedience as Worship: Keeping God's commandments is not about earning His love but about expressing our love for Him.

The Blessings of Covenant Faithfulness

Remaining faithful to God's covenant brings profound blessings. In Jeremiah 29:11, God assures us, "For I know the plans I have for you, declares the Lord, plans to prosper you and not to harm you, plans to give you hope and a future." These plans are fulfiled when we trust and obey Him.

Real-life testimony shows how covenant faithfulness transforms lives. For example, a man once struggling with addiction found freedom by surrendering to God's covenant.

Through prayer and obedience, he replaced the idols of substance abuse with the peace and joy of God's presence.

As we align our lives with God's covenant, we experience His love's security, His Spirit's guidance, and the joy of His blessings. In the next chapter, we will explore the dangers of idolatry and how recognising God's jealousy leads to a life of true freedom and fulfilment.

Chapter 4: The Danger Of Idolatry

Defining Idolatry in Modern Times

When many people think of idolatry, they imagine golden statues or ancient rituals, but idolatry is far more pervasive and subtle in modern life. At its core, idolatry is anything that takes God's rightful place in our hearts and lives. It is valuing something or someone more than God, allowing it to dominate our thoughts, choices, and actions.

In modern times, idols are often intangible but equally powerful. They can take the form of:

- **Materialism:** Pursuing wealth, possessions, or financial security above all else.
- **Success and Ambition:** Obsessing over career achievements or status at the expense of God's priorities.
- **Relationships:** Placing a spouse, children, or friends in a position that only God should occupy.
- **Entertainment:** Spending excessive time on hobbies, social media, or leisure while neglecting spiritual growth.
- **Self-Reliance:** Trusting in personal abilities, intellect, or resources instead of depending on God.

In essence, idolatry is anything that competes for the devotion and worship meant for God alone. As Paul warns in **Romans 1:25**, *"They exchanged the truth about God for a lie and worshipped and served created things rather than the Creator—who is forever praised."*

How Idolatry Impacts Our Relationship with God

Idolatry is not a harmless distraction; it fundamentally disrupts our relationship with God.

1. **Divides Our Devotion:** God desires our wholehearted worship. When idols take root, they divide our loyalty, making it impossible to love and serve Him fully. Jesus said in **Matthew 6:24**, *"No one can serve two masters. Either you will hate the one and love the other, or you will be devoted to the one and despise the other."*
2. A divided heart prevents us from experiencing the depth of God's presence and blessings. It creates a spiritual disconnection that leaves us feeling empty and restless.
3. **Leads to Spiritual Drift:** Just as the Israelites strayed from God when they worshipped the golden calf (**Exodus 32**), modern idols cause us to drift away from Him. Over time, this drift can lead to a hardened heart, making it harder to hear God's voice and follow His will.
4. **Destroys Trust in God:** Idolatry subtly replaces our dependence on God with reliance on the idol. For example, trusting in financial security over God's provision erodes our faith in His ability to meet our needs. This misplaced trust often leads to fear and anxiety, as idols cannot provide the peace and assurance that only God offers.
5. **Brings God's Discipline:** Because of His jealous love, God cannot tolerate idolatry. He will intervene, sometimes through painful discipline, to draw us back to Him. In **Deuteronomy 8:19**, God warns, *"If you ever forget the Lord your God and follow other gods and worship and bow down to them, I testify against you today that you will surely be destroyed."* God's discipline is an act of mercy, designed to save us from the destruction that idolatry brings.

Biblical Example:
The Rich Young Ruler (Matthew 19:16–22)

The story of the rich young ruler illustrates the subtle danger of idolatry. When the young man asked Jesus how to inherit eternal life, Jesus challenged him to sell his possessions and follow Him. The man's refusal revealed that his wealth hadbecome an idol, preventing him from fully surrendering to God.

This story is a cautionary tale for modern believers. We may not bow to physical idols, but when we cling to anything more tightly than we cling to God, we fall into the same trap.

Real-Life Practice:
Identifying and Overcoming Modern Idols

In everyday life, identifying idols requires honest self-reflection. Ask yourself:

- What occupies my thoughts and time the most?
- What do I fear losing the most
- Where do I turn for comfort, security, or identity?

Once we identify idols, the next step is to replace them with worship and dependence on God. Here's how:

Surrender Everything to God

Just as Abraham was willing to sacrifice Isaac, the son of promise, on Mount Moriah (**Genesis 22**), we must be willing to surrender anything that competes with God. Trust that He will provide and restore what is good for us.

Personal Reflection: A business professional once realised that her career had become an idol. She worked tirelessly, neglecting her family and spirituallife. When she surrendered her career to God, she found greater peace and balance, trusting Him to guide her work.

Cultivate Gratitude

Gratitude helps shift our focus from created things to the Creator. Thanking God for His blessings reminds us that He alone is the source of all we need.

Regularly Seek God's Presence

Spending time in prayer, Scripture, and worship helps align our hearts with God. The more we experience His presence, the less appealing idols become.

Practice Generosity

Generosity breaks the hold of materialism and self-centeredness. Giving freely demonstrates our trust in God's provision and redirects our focus to His kingdom.

Living Free from Idols

Freedom from idolatry is not about deprivation but liberation. As we cast down idols and centre our lives on God, we discover true joy, peace, and fulfilment. God's promise in **Jeremiah 29:13** is clear: *"You will seek Me and find Me when you seek Me with all your heart."*

Letting go of idols may feel difficult at first, but it is a necessary step to embrace the abundant life God has for us fully. In the next chapter, we will explore how embracing God's jealousy leads to greater intimacy with Him and transforms every aspect of our lives.

Chapter 5: Recognising Our Own Idols

Practical Steps to Identify What Competes with God in Our Lives

Identifying idols in our lives begins with intentional self-examination and a willingness to allow the Holy Spirit to reveal areas of misplaced devotion. While idols often disguise themselves as good things, such as relationships, careers, or even ministry, they become problematic when they usurp God's rightful place.

Here are practical steps to uncover what competes with God in our lives:

Ask the Hard Questions

Start by asking yourself:

- What do I think about most often?
- Where do I invest the majority of my time, energy, and resources?
- What am I most afraid of losing?
- Where do I turn for comfort, identity, or security during difficult times? These questions often highlight areas of attachment that have taken precedence over God. As Jesus said in **Matthew 6:21**, *"For where your treasure is, there your heart will be also."*
1. **Pay Attention to Emotional Reactions:** Strong emotions like anger, fear, or anxiety often indicate the presence of an idol. For example, feeling overwhelming anxiety about finances may signal that money has become an idol. By bringing these emotions to God, we can uncover the deeper issues of misplaced trust.
2. **Examine Your Priorities:** Reflect on how you spend your time. Do daily habits and decisions reflect a commitment to God's kingdom, or do they reveal competing priorities? Jesus taught in **Matthew 6:33**, *"Seek first His kingdom and His*

righteousness, and all these things will be given to you as well."
3. **Invite God to Search Your Heart:** Pray as King David did in **Psalm 139:23-24**: *"Search me, God, and know my heart; test me and know my anxious thoughts. See if there is any offensive way in me, and lead me in the way everlasting."* The Holy Spirit faithfully convicts us of anything hindering our relationship with God.
4. **Seek Counsel from Trusted Believers:** Sometimes. Others can see idols in our lives that we are blind to. Share your struggles with trusted friends, mentors, or spiritual leaders who can providebiblical guidance and encouragement.

Personal Reflection and Self-Assessment

Recognising idols requires honest reflection and a willingness to surrender. Below are a few exercises to help you assess areas that may need realignment:

1. **The Worship Inventory:** Create a list of what you value most in life. This could include family, career, possessions, hobbies, or goals. Ask yourself:
   - Does this lead me closer to God or pull me away?
   - Am I placing my trust in this rather than inGod?

Biblical Example: In **1 Kings 18:21**, Elijah confronted the Israelites, who were torn between worshipping God and Baal. He challenged them, *"How long will you waver between two opinions? If the Lord is God, follow Him; but if Baal is God, follow him."* This story reminds us to evaluate where our ultimate allegiance lies.

2. **The If Only" Test:** Complete this statement: *"If only I had, I would feel secure and happy."* Whatever fills that blank could be a potential idol. While God provides blessings, we must remember that true contentment comes from Him alone **(Philippians 4:11-13)**.
3. **The Sabbath Challenge:** Take one day to unplug from distractions and focus solely on God. Avoid work,

entertainment, or anything that normally consumes your time. This practice often reveals what competes for your attention and devotion.
4. *Real-Life Story:* A busy entrepreneur once attempted a "technology fast" as part of observing the Sabbath. She realised her constant need to check emails and social media had become an idol. By surrendering this habit to God, she found renewed peace and clarity in her relationship with Him.
5. **Confession and Accountability:** Once you identify an idol, confess it to God and ask for His help in removing it. Share your struggle with a trusted accountability partner who can support and pray for you. James 5:16 encourages us to *"confess your sins to each other and pray for each other so that you may be healed."*

Breaking Free from Idols

Recognising idols is the first step toward spiritual freedom, but it requires action to remove them. Consider these steps to re-centre your heart on God:

- **Redirect Worship to God Alone:** Begin each day by dedicating your time, work, and relationships to God. Worship Him in spirit and truth, as Jesus instructed in **John 4:24**.
- **Replace Idols with Spiritual Practices:** Replace habits that promote idolatry with practices that nurture your faith, such as prayer, Bible study, and serving others.
- **Trust God's Sufficiency:** Acknowledge that God is enough. Rest in His promises, knowing He provides everything you need for a fulfiled life (**2Peter 1:3**).

Living with God at the Center

As we identify and remove idols, we experience the freedom and joy of a life wholly devoted to God. While the process may be challenging, it leads to deeper intimacy with Him and a clearer understanding of His purpose for our lives.

In the next Chapter we will delve into the tension between worldly demands and spiritual commitments. It highlights the importance of Prioritising what truly matters, nurturing a heart aligned with faith, and finding harmony amidst life's competing responsibilities.

Chapter 6:
Competing Priorities In Our Heart

In our journey of faith, the heart often becomes a battleground for competing priorities. These are the desires, ambitions, and attachments that vie for our attention, frequently pushing God into a secondary role. The struggle between these competing forces can challenge our commitment to making God the centre of our lives. Below, we explore some of the most common priorities that often compete with our devotion to God:

Materialism and Wealth

1. **The Pursuit of Money:** In a world that places great value on financial success, the pursuit of wealth can easily overshadow our relationship with God. When we prioritise material possessions or the pursuit of financial security, we risk focusing on accumulation rather than spiritual growth. Jesus warned against this in Matthew 6:24: *"No one can serve two masters. Either you will hate the one and love the other, or you will be devoted to the one and despise the other."*
2. **The Temptation:** A life focused on wealth may shift our trust from God's provision to our own ability to acquire material goods, making possessions take precedence over the Creator.

Career and Ambition

1. **Work as an Idol:** The ambition to succeed in our careers can dominate our lives. Long hours, pressure for promotions, and a desire for recognition can lead us to neglect our spiritual health, relationships, and well-being.
2. **The Challenge:** Jesus reminded us in Matthew 6:33: *"Seek first His kingdom and His righteousness, and all these things will be given to you as well."* This teaches that our relationship with God should always come before our career aspirations.

Relationships

1. **Idolatry of Relationships:** Whether romantic, familial, or friendships, our relationships can sometimes become more important than our relationship with God. When our desire for love or approval from others becomes our primary goal, it can cloud our judgment, causing us to elevate human affection above divine obedience.
2. **The Caution:** Jesus addressed this in Luke 14:26: *"If anyone comes to me and does not hate father and mother, wife and children, brothers and sisters—yes, even their ownlife—such a person cannot be my disciple."* This verse emphasizes that our devotion to God must surpass all other relationships, highlighting the need to prioritize God above everything.

Social Media and Entertainment

1. **The Distraction of Instant Gratification:** In an age of constant connectivity and immediate entertainment, we may spend more time scrolling through social media or binge-watching shows than engaging in spiritual practices like prayer and Bible reading.
2. **The Struggle:** These distractions often fail to satisfy our deeper spiritual needs. Psalm 37:4 reminds us: *"Delight yourself in the Lord, and He will give you the desires of your heart."* True fulfilment comes from prioritizing God's presence over transient distractions.

Self-Centeredness

1. **The Temptation to Focus on Ourselves:** Our culture often encourages self-interest, where comfort, convenience, and personal desires can outweigh the call to serve God and others. This self-centeredness can hinder spiritual growth and hinder our connection with God.
2. **The Call to Die to Self:** In Mark 8:34, Jesus calls us to *"takeup our cross and follow Me."* True discipleship requires

surrendering our own will to God's purpose and Prioritizing His plans over our personal desires.

Pride and Reputation

1. **The Need for Approval:** Our desire to maintain a certain image or gain approval from others can compete with our commitment to God. The pursuit of recognition or social status may lead us to prioritize our public persona over the development of our spiritual life.
2. **The Warning:** Proverbs 29:25 says: *"The fear of man lays a snare, but whoever trusts in the Lord is safe."* The desire for human approval can trap us into compromising ourvalues and losing sight of God's call for our lives.

Comfort and Convenience

1. **Avoiding Discomfort:** Seeking ease and avoidingchallenging situations can take precedence over following God's calling, especially when it requires sacrifice or discomfort.
2. **The Truth:** Jesus never promised an easy journey but encouraged us to follow Him despite the challenges. In Matthew 7:14, He said, *"But small is the gate and narrow the road that leads to life, and only a few find it."* True discipleship often involves difficulty, but it leads to eternal rewards.

Success and Achievement

1. **The Pursuit of Accomplishments:** Striving for success can become an idol when it's pursued at the expense of our relationship with God. While striving for achievement is not wrong, when it becomes our ultimate goal, we risk losing sight of God's purpose for us.
2. **The Perspective:** In Philippians 3:8, Paul declares: *"I consider everything a loss because of the surpassing worth of knowing Christ Jesus my Lord."* True success is found inour relationship with Christ, not in worldly achievements.

Pleasure and Comfort

1. **The Allure of Pleasure:** The pursuit of pleasure—whether through food, entertainment, or luxury—can become a competing priority when it replaces our pursuit of God's presence.
2. **The Warning:** 1 John 2:16 cautions: *"For everything in the world—the lust of the flesh, the lust of the eyes, and the pride of life—comes not from the Father but from the world."* Pursuing fleeting pleasures leads us away from the lasting joy found in God.

Removing Idols and Making God the Centre

Embracing the journey of setting aside worldly idols and placing God at the centre of our worship is a continuous and heartfelt act of intentional devotion. It requires self-reflection, surrender, and consistentaction. Here's how we can recommit to God:

1. **Acknowledge the Presence of Idols:** Recognise what competes with God for your heart—be it money, career, relationships, or comfort. Honest self-reflection is key.

Action Step: Ask God to reveal any idols in your heart through prayer. *Psalm 139:23-24* offers a powerful prayer: *"Search me, O God, and know my heart..."*

2. **Repent and Surrender:** Repentance involves turning away from what has taken God's place and surrendering those areas to Him.

Action Step: In prayer, confess your misplaced priorities and surrender them to God, trusting Him with every part of your life.

3. **Recommit to Exclusive Worship:** Choose God daily, in every situation, as your highest priority. Worship is a lifestyle, not limited to certain moments.

Action Step: Dedicate time daily for prayer, Bible reading, and worship. Begin each day seeking God and committing to prioritize Him.

4. **Align Your Priorities with God's Will:** Allow God to shape your priorities, seeking His guidance in every area of life— relationships, career, finances, and more.

Action Step: Regularly ask, "Is this decision aligned with God's will?" Let His Word guide your choices. *Matthew 6:33* urges: *"Seek first His kingdom..."*

5. **Fill Your Heart with God's Word:** The Bible transforms our hearts and keeps us focused on God. When we immerse ourselves in Scripture, we are reminded of His faithfulness and love.

Action Step: Commit to daily Bible study and meditation, allowing God's truth to guide your thoughts and actions.

6. **Surround Yourself with a Supportive Community:** Engage with others who encourage you to keep God first. Accountability and shared wisdom help maintain focus.

Action Step: Participate in a local church or Bible study group, building relationships that foster your spiritual growth.

7. **Trust in God's Promises:** Trust that as you seek God first, He will provide for your needs and guide your life according to His perfect will.

Action Step: Reflect on God's promises, like *Philippians 4:19 "And my God will meet all your needs..."* standing firm in faith that He will never fail you.

Conclusion

These competing priorities, though not inherently wrong, can crowd out God if we're not intentional about placing Him at the centre of our lives. As Jesus reminds us in Matthew 6:21: "For where your treasure is, there your heart will be also." The challenge for every believer is to examine where our heart is truly invested. If anything competes with God for our devotion, we must realign our priorities, placing Him first— because He alone is worthy of our undivided worship and devotion.

In the next chapter, we will explore how embracing God's jealousy can transform our priorities and bring spiritual alignment. Let us remember the words of the Apostle John in 1 John 5:21: "Dear children, keep yourselves from idol.

Chapter 7: God's Call to Holiness

The Call to Live a Life Set Apart for God

From the very beginning, God's desire for His people has been to live lives that reflect His holiness. The Bible is filled with reminders that God's people are called to be set apart, to live differently from the world, and to reflect His nature in all areas of life. This call to holiness is not about perfection but about alignment with God's heart and purpose for our lives.

In **1 Peter 1:16**, God commands, *"Be holy, because I am holy."* This is not a suggestion but a direct call for His people to mirror His character. Holiness, in this context, means being consecrated, dedicated, and distinct from the ways of the world. The Hebrew word for holy, *qadosh*, refers to something that is set apart for sacred use, something devoted entirely to God.

This call to holiness is not just about external behavior but involves the transformation of the heart. **Romans 12:1-2** tells us that our worship to God is a living sacrifice, and we are not to conform to the patterns of this world but to be transformed by the renewing of our minds. Holiness begins in the heart, as God works within us to bring about His righteousness.

Embracing God's Standard for Purity and Devotion

Living a holy life means embracing God's standard for purity, not the standards set by culture or society. God calls us to purity in every aspect of life: our thoughts, words, actions, and relationships. This can be challenging in a world that often promotes self-gratification and compromise, but it is God's design for His people.

1. **Purity of Heart and Mind:** Jesus made it clear in **Matthew 5:8**: *"Blessed are the pure in heart, for they will see God."*

Holiness begins in the heart, where the purity of our thoughts and desires shapes our behaviour. The battle for holiness is often fought in our minds. We are called to take every thought captive to make it obedient to Christ (**2 Corinthians 10:5**).

Practical Example: One individual struggling with impure thoughts turned to scripture for help. They memorised verses like **Philippians 4:8** ("Whatever is pure, lovely, admirable—think about such things") and began replacing unholy thoughts with thoughts centred on Christ. Over time, their thinking became realigned with God's truth, and their actions followed suit.

2. **Purity in Relationships:** God's call to holiness is reflected in how we treat others. This includes living out the fruit of the Spirit, such as love, patience, kindness, and self-control (**Galatians 5:22-23**). In relationships, purity involves respecting others and honouring God's design for sexuality, marriage, and friendship.

   Biblical Example: The story of Joseph in **Genesis 39** demonstrates purity in relationships. When faced with the temptation to sin with Potiphar's wife, Joseph made a deliberate choice to flee from sin, saying, *"How then could I do such a wicked thing and sin against God?"* (Genesis 39:9). His decision reflects a heart devoted to God's standard of purity, even in the face of temptation.

3. *Purity in Speech and Action:* Holiness also includes purity in what we speak and how we act. **Ephesians 4:29** teaches that *"Do not let any unwholesome talk come out of your mouths, but only what is helpful for building others up according to their needs, that it may benefit those who listen."* Our words should reflect God's love, truth, and grace.

   Practical Example: A business professional faced a choice: to use cutting-edge but deceptive practices to close a deal or to act with integrity. He chose integrity, even though it meant walking away from a lucrative opportunity. His commitment to holiness in his actions stood as a testimony to his faith in God's standard, even in the market place.

4. **Purity in Worship and Devotion:** The essence of holiness is wholehearted devotion to God. This involves Prioritizing God in our lives, and setting aside time for prayer, worship, and reflection. It also means eliminating distractions that take our attention away from Him. **Matthew 22:37** calls us to love the Lord our God with all our heart, soul, and mind. True devotion is undivided—God is not to share the throne of our hearts with anything else.

Real-Life Example: A woman in a leadership role often found herself torn between her commitments to work, family, and ministry. She began setting aside time each morning for personal worship and prayer before starting her day. This practice helped her focus her heart on God first, allowing her to live more intentionally and with greater peace, knowing she was aligning her life with God's will.

The Transforming Power of Holiness

The call to holiness is not just a command; it's an invitation to experience God's best for our lives. As we align our hearts with Him, we begin to experience true freedom. **John 8:36** promises, *"So if the Son sets you free, you will be free indeed."* Holiness is about setting ourselves apart for God's purposes, but it also results in spiritual freedom. The more we live in alignment with God's will, the more we experience His peace, joy, and presence.

Living a holy life is not about legalistic rules; it is about becoming more like Christ. In **Romans 8:29**, we are told that God's ultimate purpose for us is to be conformed to the image of His Son. As we pursue holiness, we reflect the character of Christ and invite others to experience the transforming power of His love.

Real-Life Story:
A Life of Holiness Transformed

A woman shared her testimony of how God transformed her life as she embraced His call to holiness. Coming from a background of broken relationships and unhealthy habits, she struggled with the idea of living differently. But when she began to read God's Word and seek His heart for her life, she felt the deep conviction of His holiness.

Over time, she let go of toxic relationships, changed her career to align with her values, and committed to living a life that honoured God. Her transformation wasn't instant, but she found joy and peace as she allowed God's standards to shape her life. Through her journey, she became a living testimony of the power of God's call to holiness.

Conclusion

God's call to holiness is a call to live fully for Him—to live a life set apart, devoted to His purposes. It is not always easy,

but it is always worth it. As we embrace God's standard for purity and devotion, we open ourselves to His transforming power and experience the fullness of life that He promises. Remember, holiness is not about perfection but about a heart surrendered to God. Let us, as His people, continue to walk in His ways, shining His light in a world that desperately needs it.

The next Chapter evaluates what has taken precedence over our relationship with God. It will provide actionable steps to refocus worship and encourage you to find joy in a life centred on Him.

This chapter serves as a powerful reminder that exclusive worship is not about restriction but about freedom—freedom to live fully in the peace, joy, and purpose that comes from honouring God above all else.

Chapter 8:
Exclusive Worship in Modern Times

Understanding the Need for Exclusive Worship in a World Full of Distractions

We live in a world that is constantly vying for our attention—through the incessant buzz of notifications, the pressure of societal expectations, and the lure of materialism. Every day, we are bombarded with distractions that challenge our focus and shift our priorities. In such anenvironment, maintaining exclusive worship of God becomes a counter-cultural act, one that requires intentionality and purpose.

Exodus 34:14 speaks to the heart of this issue: *"Do not worship any other god, for the Lord, whose name is Jealous, is a jealous God."* This call to exclusive worship was not just for the Israelites in ancient times; it is as relevant today as it was then. The distraction of false gods in the form of technology, success, relationships, and self-satisfaction has only grown in the modern world. It is easy to allow these things to take the place of our devotion to God, even subtly, without realising it.

Exclusive worship involves more than just participating in church services or singing worship songs; it is a posture of the heart that says, "God, you are my ultimate priority. Nothing else compares to You." In a society that offers so many alternatives for fulfilment and success, the call to exclusive worship challenges us to evaluate what truly holds the throne of our hearts. **Matthew 6:24** makes this clear: *"No one can serve two masters... You cannot serve both God and money."* This is a timeless principle—our loyalty and devotion must be singular.

The Importance of Prioritising God Over Everything Else

The practice of exclusive worship is a deliberate decision to place God at the centre of our lives, ahead of everything else. It means choosing His will, His ways, and His priorities above all others, even when it requires sacrifice or discomfort.

1. **Worship Beyond Sunday Services:** In the hustle of everyday life, it can be easy to compartmentalize our faith, dedicating Sunday mornings to worship while the rest of the week is filled with our personal agendas. However, **Romans 12:1** calls us to offer our bodies as a living sacrifice, holy and pleasing to God, which is our true and proper worship. Exclusive worship involves aligning our lives with God's values every day. Whether at work, with family, or in leisure, the goal is to honour God in all that we do.

   Practical Example: A corporate executive decided to prioritize his faith in every area of life. Every day before work, he spent time in prayer and reflection, seeking God's guidance for his meetings, decisions, and interactions. By integrating his worship into his daily routine, he saw significant changes not only in his personal life but in the way he approached his leadership role. His decisions were more aligned with his values, and his actions became a testimony of God's presence in the workplace

2. *Time Management and Spiritual Priorities:* In a world that demands more of our time than ever before, exclusive worship requires intentional management of our time. **Psalm 90:12** encourages us: *"Teach us to number our days, that we may gain a heart of wisdom."* Time is a precious commodity, and how we spend it reveals what we value most. The way we prioritize our time speaks volumes about where our true affections lie.

   Real-Life Example: A young mother, overwhelmed by the demands of raising young children, realized that she was neglecting her time with God. After reflecting on her priorities, she began setting aside early mornings for prayer and Bible study before the rest of her day began. This time with God brought peace, joy, and purpose, helping her navigate her busy life with greater wisdom and grace. Her exclusive worship of God became the foundation of her day, influencing her relationship with her family and her approach to motherhood.

3. **Worship Through Sacrifice:** To worship exclusively means to offer sacrifices. These sacrifices might not always be physical, but they can involve letting go of certain comforts, desires, or distractions in order to give God more of our time, attention, and energy. Jesus taught in **Luke 9:23**, *"Whoever wants to be my disciple must deny themselves and take up their cross daily and follow me."* The practice of exclusive worship sometimes calls us to make hard choices, like turning down an opportunity that conflicts with our faith or choosing simplicity over consumerism. These sacrifices, while difficult, draw us closer to God and teach us the depths of His love.

    Practical Example: A successful entrepreneur felt the pull of work taking precedence over his relationship with God. Realizing that his business was consuming too much of his time and energy, he made the difficult decision to scale back his hours and spend more time serving in his church and with his family. His sacrifice was not just in the practical sense but in his surrender of his ambitions to God's purposes. He found that by Prioritizing worship overwork, he was able to experience deeper fulfilment and peace.

4. **Focusing on Eternal** Values: One of the greatest distractions to exclusive worship is the fleeting nature of worldly pursuits. **Matthew 6:19-21** reminds us not to store up treasures on earth but to focus on treasures in heaven. The pursuit of money, fame, status, or even relationships can easily pull our attention away from God's eternal kingdom. We are called to shift our focus from temporal gains to eternal rewards, finding our true joy in serving God and fulfiling His will.

Real-Life Example: A young man, seeking approval from his peers and society, invested all his energy in climbing the corporate ladder. However, despite his success, he felt an inner emptiness. After attending a retreat focused on living for God's purposes, he realized that he had been chasing after the wrong things. He shifted his focus to serving others and building relationships rooted in faith, discovering lasting joy in the process.

Exclusive Worship: A Lifestyle of Devotion

Exclusive worship is not a one-time decision; it is a lifestyle of devotion. It means consistently choosing to honour God in every area of life. It is a daily act of surrender and a conscious decision to keep God at the centre. As we make Him our first priority, everything else falls into place **Matthew 22:37** calls us to love God with all our heart, soul, and mind. This is not merely a command; it is an invitation to experience life to its fullest, in a way that aligns with God's will and purpose. True worship is an act of love, and love always prioritizes the object of its affection. When we love God above all else, everything else in our lives will be shaped by that

Conclusion

In a world full of distractions, the call to exclusive worship is a radical one. It requires us to prioritize God over everything else, to make Him the center of our lives, and to live out our faith in all that we do. As we embrace this call, we experience a deeper relationship with God and a more fulfiling life. Exclusive worship is not just about what we do in church; it is about how we live each day, making God our highest priority and living in obedience to His will. By doing so, we align ourselves with His eternal purposes and experience the fullness of His presence.

The next chapter encourages us to evaluate our current habits of prayer and Bible study, offering practical ways to grow in both areas.

By the end of this next chapter, we will feel equipped and inspired to make prayer and Scripture an integral part of our daily lives, unlocking the joy and peace that come from a vibrant, personal relationship with God.

Chapter 9:
The Role of Prayer and Scripture

How to Develop a Strong Prayer Life and Engage with the Bible

A vibrant, exclusive relationship with God is deeply rooted in prayer and the study of His Word. As we navigate life's complexities, both prayer and Scripture serve as the primary means of communicating with God, understanding His will, and growing in faith. In a world that often prioritises busyness and distractions, developing a strong prayer life and a consistent engagement with the Bible are vital for maintaining an exclusive worship lifestyle.

The Foundation of Prayer Communication with God

Prayer is the heart-to-heart communication between God and His people. It is more than just speaking to God; it is a conversation that involves both speaking and listening. **Philippians 4:6-7** encourages us to bring our anxieties before God in prayer, with thanksgiving, and to receive His peace in return: *"Do not be anxious about anything, but in every situation, by prayer and petition, with thanksgiving, present your requests to God. And the peace of God, which transcends all understanding, will guard your hearts and your minds in Christ Jesus."* Prayer fosters intimacy with God, as we share our concerns, hopes, and struggles with Him. But prayer also allows us to listen, allowing God's still, small voice to guide us. Just as any healthy relationship thrives on both communication and active listening, our relationship with God flourishes when we give time to listen for His voice in the quiet moments of prayer.

Practical Steps to Build a Strong Prayer Life

1. **Set Aside Dedicated Time for Prayer:** It is essential to set aside specific times each day to pray. This discipline allows prayer to become a priority and prevents it from being relegated to mere moments of crisis. For example, Jesus modelled this discipline in **Mark 1:35**, where He rose early in the morning to spend time in prayer. Setting a specific time each day, even if just for a few minutes, helps to establish consistency in our communication with God.
2. **Be Honest and Authentic in Prayer:** Prayer is not about fancy words or pretentious phrases; it is about being honest with God. **Psalm 62:8** invites us: *"Trust in him at all times, you people; pour out your hearts to him, for God is our refuge."* We are encouraged to pour out our hearts before God, expressing our deepest emotions, desires, and fears. Whether in moments of joy or sorrow, prayer allows us to be raw and vulnerable with the One who knows us best.
3. **Incorporate Praise and Thanksgiving:** Even in difficult circumstances, **1 Thessalonians 5:16-18** encourages us to pray continually, give thanks in all circumstances, and rejoice. As we pray, we should always remember to praise God for who He is and thank Him for His blessings. This practice shifts our focus away from our struggles and towards His goodness, fueling a heart of worship.

The Power of Spending Time with God in His Word

Just as prayer is essential for communicating with God, the Bible is vital for understanding His heart, His will, and His promises. **Psalm 119:105** reminds us, *"Your word is a lamp for my feet, a light on my path."* The Bible is not just a historical document; it is God's living Word, meant to guide, teach, and transform us.

Spending time in God's Word reveals His character and deepens our understanding of His desires for us. It is through Scripture that we learn how to live a life that honours God and practices exclusive worship.

Every book, chapter, and verse in the Bible points to the overarching story of God's redemptive love for humanity and reveals His desire for a devoted relationship with us.

Practical Steps for Engaging with Scripture:

1. **Make Bible Reading Daily Habit:** In order to grow in our knowledge of God's Word, it is essential to set aside time each day for reading the Bible. Just as we need daily food to nourish our bodies, we need daily engagement with Scripture to nourish our souls. You can start with a chapter a day or follow a Bible reading plan. The key is consistency. Even in moments when it feels difficult, the act of showing up daily is vital for spiritual growth.
2. **Meditate on** Scripture Joshua **1:8:** teaches us to meditate on the Word of God day and night: *"Keep this Book of the Law always on your lips; meditate on it day and night, so that you may be careful to do everything written in it."* Meditation on Scripture involves reflecting deeply on God's Word, allowing it to permeate our minds and hearts. This practice enables us to understand and apply His principles to our lives.
3. **Apply the Word to Your Life James 1:22** challenges us to be doers of the Word, not just hearers. As we read and meditate on Scripture, it is essential to actively apply what we learn. Whether through making better decisions, changing our attitudes, or growing in faith, Scripture has the power to transform us when we allow it to shape our actions.

Prayer and Scripture as Partners in Worship

While prayer allows us to communicate with God, Scriptureallows us to hear from Him. Both are integral to an exclusiverelationship with God. When we spend time in prayer and Scripture, we open ourselves to a deeper connection with God. In this time, we align our hearts and minds with His, cultivating a worshipful life that honours Him. Jesus Himself modelled this life of devotion. In **Matthew 4:4**, when He was tempted by the enemy in the wilderness, He responded with the words, *"Man shall not live on bread alone, but on every word that comes from* *the mouth of God."* Jesus shows us that the Word of God is our true sustenance and that our worship is shaped not only by our prayers but by how deeply we engage with the truths He has given us.

Real-Life Example: The Power of Prayer and Scripture in Transformation

A woman struggling with anxiety and uncertainty found herself drawn into a deep prayer and Bible study habit. She began to pray each morning, surrendering her fears and concerns to God, while simultaneously studying passages on peace and trust in His sovereignty. Over time, she began to notice a significant change. Her fears were replaced with a deep sense of peace, and her heart became more attuned to God's voice. By embracing prayer and Scripture as tools for exclusive worship, she was able to surrender her anxieties to God and trust in His plan. The power of prayer and the truths of Scripture worked together to transform her mindset, deepen her relationship with God, and bring peace into her life.

Conclusion

Prayer and Scripture are essential components of living a life of exclusive worship. Through prayer, we communicate with God and develop an intimate relationship with Him. Through Scripture, we gain insight into His heart and understand His will for our lives. Together, they empower usto grow spiritually, align our hearts with God's, and live outHis call to wholehearted devotion. When we prioritize time with God in both prayer and His Word, we open ourselves up to a transformative relationship that guides us into deeper worship, peace, and purpose.

The next chapter, Chapter 10 focuses on the transformative journey of surrendering every area of life to God. Readers will explore the challenges of letting go of control, the peace that comes from trusting in God's plan, and practical ways to live in alignment with His will.

Chapter 10: Surrendering to God's Will

How to Surrender Every Area of Your Life to God

Surrendering to God's will is one of the most profound expressions of exclusive worship. It is the act of laying down our own desires, plans, and control to fully embrace His perfect will for our lives. This process requires trust, humility, and a willingness to submit every area of our lives—our relationships, careers, finances, health, and personal ambitions—into God's hands. Surrendering to God's will is not a one-time event but a continuous act of submission, where we choose to follow His leading over our own.

The Bible calls us to surrender ourselves to God in several key ways. **Romans 12:1-2** encourages us to offer our bodies as a living sacrifice, holy and pleasing to God, which is our true act of worship. *"Therefore, I urge you, brothers and sisters, in view of God's mercy, to offer your bodies as a living sacrifice, holy and pleasing to God—this is your true and proper worship. Do not conform to the pattern of this world, but be transformed by the renewing of your mind. Then you will be able to test and approve what God's will is—His good, pleasing, and perfect will."*

The invitation to surrender our lives begins with a heart posture of worship—recognising that we belong to God and that every aspect of our lives is under His sovereignty. Our surrender is not a be grudging submission but an act of love and trust in the One who knows what is best for us.

Steps to Surrender Every Area of Your Life

1. **Acknowledge God's Sovereignty:** Surrender starts with acknowledging that God is in control. **Proverbs 3:5-6** teach us to trust in the Lord with all our hearts and not lean on our own understanding. In every area of our lives, we must remind

ourselves that God's plans are higher and better than ours. The sooner we embrace this truth, the easier it becomes to surrender everything to Him.

2. **Identify Areas of Control:** Many of us hold onto certain aspects of our lives tightly—our finances, relationships, or career path. The first step in surrender is recognising these areas where we are still trying to control outcomes. Reflecton your life and ask God to reveal areas where you have yet to fully trust Him. Is there a part of your life you are holding back from God? Surrender means releasing that area into His hands, trusting that He will lead and guide you according to His will.

3. **Submit Your Desires and Plans James 4:13-15:** reminds us that we should not boast about our plans without recognising God's ultimate authority: *"Now listen, you who say, 'Today or tomorrow we will go to this or that city, spend a year there, carry on business and make money.' Why, you do not even know what will happen tomorrow. What is your life? You are a mist that appears for a little while and then vanishes. Instead, you ought to say, 'If it is the Lord's will, we will live and do this or that."* Surrender involves letting go of our own agenda and submitting our plans to God's purposes, acknowledging that His will is always best.

4. **Pray for Strength to Surrender:** Surrendering to God is a process that requires daily surrender and dependence on Him. **Luke 22:42** shows us Jesus' example of surrender in the Garden of Gethsemane, when He prayed, *"Father, if you are willing, take this cup from me; yet not my will, but yours be done."* Like Jesus, we must pray for the strength to surrender our will and accept God's will, even when it is difficult or doesn't align with our own desires.

Letting Go of Control and Trusting in God's Plan

Trusting in God's plan is a continual act of faith. While surrender is about yielding control, trusting God's plan involves resting in the certainty that He is trustworthy and that His plan is good, even when we don't understand it. The idea of control is an illusion—we may think we have control over our lives, but the reality is that God is always in control. When we relinquish our need to control, we free ourselves to walk in the freedom of trusting God.

One of the key passages that illustrates the importance of letting go of control is **Jeremiah 29:11**, where God promises: *"For I know the plans I have for you," declares the Lord, "plans to prosper you and not to harm you, plans to give you a hope and a future."* This verse is a reminder that God's plans for us are filled with hope and a future, even when the journey is challenging.

Steps to Let Go of Control and Trust God's Plan

1. **Recognise the Limitations of Your Control:** The first step in trusting God's plan is acknowledging that we cannot control everything. Life is full of uncertainties, and we often face circumstances beyond our control. **Matthew 6:27** reminds us, *"Can any one of you by worrying add a single hour to your life?"* Worry and control are futile attempts to manage what only God can handle. Acknowledging our limitations frees us to trust in God's ability to handle everything according to His perfect will.
2. **Embrace the Unknown with Faith:** Surrendering to God's will often means walking into the unknown. We may not have all the answers, and the path ahead may not be clear. **2 Corinthians 5:7** reminds us, *"For we live by faith, not by sight."* We are called to trust in God's leading, even when we cannot see the whole picture. Trusting God's plan requires embracing the uncertainty of life and walking forward with faith, knowing that He will guide us step by step.
3. **Release Your Fears and Anxiety:** Trusting in God's plan requires letting go of fear and anxiety. **1 Peter 5:7** encourages us to cast all our anxiety on Him because He cares for us. When we surrender to God's will, we release our fears about the future, our insecurities, and our concerns. Trusting God brings

peace, knowing He is in control and His plan is always for our good.

Real-Life Example: Surrendering to God's Will

A young man named David had big plans for his career in the corporate world. He worked long hours, sacrificed his personal life, and strived for success. However, despite his hard work, he felt unfulfiled and disconnected from God. He eventually realized that his career ambitions had become an idol, taking priority over his relationship with God. After a season of prayer and reflection, David felt the Lord calling him to leave his corporate job and pursue a ministry career that he had never considered before. This decision was daunting and filled him with fear about the future, but he chose to surrender his career plans to God's will.

As David took this step of faith, he saw God's provision and guidance in ways he had never imagined. His new ministry brought him greater fulfilment, peace, and a deeper connection with God. By surrendering control and trusting God's plan, David found a purpose that was far greater than his own ambitions.

Conclusion

Surrendering to God's will is a powerful act of worship that allows us to relinquish control and trust in His perfect plan. It is an ongoing process that involves offering every area of our lives to God, submitting our desires to His will, and trusting that He will lead us in the right direction. As we surrender, we begin to experience the peace that comes from knowing that God's plan is always better than our own. Letting go of control is not about losing freedom; it's about finding true freedom in trusting the One who created us and knows what is best for us. Through surrender, we embrace God's love, guidance, and purpose, leading us into a profound and more more intimate relationship with Him.

Jealous For You

Next Chapter celebrates the depth of God's passionate, jealous love, which desires the best for His people. Chapter 11 explores how fully embracing God's love transforms our lives and brings joy and fulfilment through wholehearted devotion.

Chapter 11:
The Beauty of God's Jealous Love

Celebrating the Depth of God's Love That Desires the Best for Us

The love of God is truly beyond comprehension. It is not a passive or self-serving love but one that is deep, active, and transformational. **God's jealousy** for us is rooted in His passionate, unwavering love— He desires the best for us, and His heart yearns for our devotion. His love is not possessive or controlling but deeply protective, caring, and desiring our highest good. When we embrace His exclusive love, we enter into a relationship where He, as our Creator and Father, seeks only what is most fulfilling and life-giving for us. In **Exodus 34:14**, God declares, *"Do not worship any other god, for the Lord, whose name is Jealous, is a jealous God."* God's "jealous" nature is not based on insecurity but on His deep commitment to our well-being. He knows that we are left with emptiness when we pursue other "gods" or distractions. His jealousy for us is a reflection of His love that wants us to experience true joy, peace, and purpose. As a loving Father, He does not want us to miss the abundant life He has for us. This divine jealousy is ultimately an expression of God's covenant love, which He demonstrated to His people throughout Scripture. **Deuteronomy 7:9** reveals, "Know therefore *that the Lord your God is God; He is the faithful God, keeping His covenant of love to a thousand generations of those who love Him and keep His commandments."* God's love for us is unshakable, rooted in His faithfulness and His desire to bless us with His best.

The depth of God's love is evident throughout the Bible, from His covenant promises to the sacrificial love displayed through Jesus Christ. **John 3:16** reminds us of the greatest demonstration of love: *"For God so loved the world that He gave His one and only Son, that whoever believes in Him shall not perish but have eternal life."* Jesus' sacrificial death on the cross was the ultimate expression of God's jealousy for our hearts—He was willing to give up everything to bring us back into a relationship with Him. Understanding this love transforms how we view God's commands and His desire for our exclusive worship. We begin to see that God's love is not about restriction but protection and offering a life far more fulfiling than anything the world can offer.

The Joy of Living Fully Devoted to God

Living fully devoted to God is not a burden or a sacrifice but a pathway to the greatest joy and fulfilment. When we align our lives with His will and love, we experience the beauty of what it means to live according to our true purpose. The more we embrace God's love, the more we are able to love and live for Him with our whole hearts. This devotion is not about mere duty or obligation but about living out God's love into our lives.

Psalm 37:4 invites us to *"Delight yourself in the Lord, and He will give you the desires of your heart."* This verse reveals the beauty of devotion to God—it's about finding joy in Him and discovering that as we live in alignment with His will, our deepest desires align with His. The more we give ourselves to God, the more we find that He satisfies our hearts in ways we never thought possible Living fully devoted to God brings a profound sense of peace. **Philippians 4:7** promises that when we surrender our lives to Him, *"the peace of God, which transcends all understanding, will guard your hearts and your minds in Christ Jesus."* There is a peace that only comes when we are wholly devoted to God—when we are not distracted by idols, worries, or competing desires, but focused on Him alone. This peace surpasses any understanding because it is rooted in the certainty that we are loved and protected by the Creator of the universe.

Additionally, living devoted to God fills our lives with purpose. **Matthew 6:33** teaches us to *"Seek first His kingdom and His righteousness, and all these things will be given to you as well."* When we make God our highest priority, our lives take on a new sense of meaning. Every action, relationship, and decision becomes an opportunity to honour and serve Him. This devotion turns the mundane intothe sacred and the ordinary into the extraordinary.

The beauty of God's jealous love is that it calls us into a life of fullness. **John 10:10** reminds us that *"I have come that they may have life, and have it to the full."* God desires for us to live fully—spiritually, emotionally, relationally, and physically—through our devotion to Him. His love is not restricting; it is life-giving.

Real-Life Experience: A Testimony of Devotion

Sarah, a young woman in her mid-thirties, had spent much of her life chasing after success, relationships, and material possessions. For years, she thought these things would bringer happiness. Yet, despite her achievements, she often felt empty and unfulfiled. It was only when Sarah gave her heartfully to God that she discovered the true joy of living for Him. She had always believed in God but never fully surrendered her life to Him, trying to maintain control over her own plans.

One day, after a series of life struggles, Sarah devoted herself completely to God. She spent time in prayer,asking God to reveal His will for her and trusting Him with her future. Through this process of surrender, she found herself experiencing a deep sense of peace and joy that she had never known before. Relationships became more meaningful, her work took on a new purpose, and she felt a deep connection with God that filled her heart. She realized that the love and devotion God was calling her to were not.

burdens, but keys to a life that was rich with joy and fulfilment.

Sarah's life transformed as she discovered that devotion to God brought her the very desires of her heart—not in the way the world defines success, but in the way God intended.She found joy not in what she had accumulated but in the relationship she cultivated with the One who loved herfiercely and exclusively.

Conclusion:
The Beauty of God's Jealous Love

God's jealous love for us is not about controlling or punishing us; it is a passionate, selfless love that desires thebest for us. His jealousy is rooted in His longing for us to experience true life, joy, peace, and fulfilment. When we respond to His love with wholehearted devotion, we enter into a life that is rich and full in ways the world cannot offer. Living fully devoted to God is not a sacrifice, but the most beautiful and fulfiling way to experience life to the fullest. God's love is pure, holy, and perfect—when we embrace it, we are transformed from the inside out, discovering the depth of joy that comes from living in His presence and according to His will.

Chapter 12: Overcoming the Struggle of Divided Loyalties

The Challenge of Competing Priorities and How to Overcome Them

In today's fast-paced world, we are constantly bombarded with competing priorities—family, work, finances, friendships, and the endless demands of life. While many of these priorities are necessary and good, they can easily overshadow our commitment to God if we are not intentional. The struggle of divided loyalties is not new; it has been a human challenge since the beginning of time. Scripture speaks to this struggle and offers guidance on how to overcome it

In **Matthew 6:24**, Jesus clearly warns, "No one can serve two masters. Either you will hate the one and love the other, or you will be devoted to the one and despise the other. You cannot serve both God and money." While this passage specifically addresses the pull of materialism, it applies broadly to any priority that competes with God's rightful place in our hearts. Divided loyalties lead to confusion, frustration, and spiritual stagnation.

In the Old Testament, the Israelites often struggled with divided loyalties. They were called to worship God alone, yet time and again they turned to idols and false gods. **1 Kings 18:21** captures the prophet Elijah confronting their wavering hearts: "How long will you waver between two opinions? If the Lord is God, follow Him; but if Baal is God, follow him." Elijah's words challenge us today: if we truly believe God is our source of life, joy, and purpose, then we must fully devote ourselves to Him and refuse to let competing priorities take His place.

Practical Strategies for Staying Committed to God

Daily Self Examination

One of the first steps to overcoming divided loyalties is to regularly examine our hearts and priorities. **Psalm 139:23-24** invites God's searching gaze: "Search me, God, and know my heart; test me and know my anxious thoughts. See if there is any offensive way in me, and lead me in the way everlasting." Spend time in prayer and reflection, asking God to reveal areas where your priorities may have shifted away from Him.

Practical Tip: At the end of each day, ask yourself, "What occupied most of my thoughts and energy today? Did I prioritise God in my decisions?"

Set Clear Boundaries

Divided loyalties often arise when we fail to set boundaries. Whether it's work overtaking family time or hobbies encroaching on spiritual practices, boundaries help protect our priorities. **Ecclesiastes 3:1** reminds us, "There is a time for everything, and a season for every activity under the heavens." God desires us to have balanced lives where He is the foundation upon which all else is built.

Practical Tip: Create a weekly schedule that intentionally includes time for prayer, Bible study, worship, and rest. Limit activities that pull you away from God and align your commitments with His values.

Prioritise the Sabbath

The Sabbath is a God-given gift designed to re-center our lives around Him. Observing the Sabbath helps us step away from distractions and realign our hearts. **Exodus 20:8** commands, "Remember the Sabbath day by keeping it holy." By dedicating time each week to focus on God, we cultivate spiritual renewal and strengthen our commitment to Him.

Practical Tip: Use your Sabbath to unplug from technology, spend time in worship, and reflect on God's blessings. Let it be a day of restoration and connection with Him.

Anchor Yourself in the Word

Divided loyalties often stem from being influenced by worldly values. Immersing ourselves in God's Word helps us stay focused on Him. **Psalm 119:105** declares, "Your word is a lamp to my feet and a light for my path." Scripture is our guide, reminding us of God's priorities and promises.

Practical Tip: Commit to reading or meditating on a passage of Scripture daily. Use Bible apps or devotionals to help you stay consistent.

Surround Yourself with Godly Community

Accountability is vital in overcoming divided loyalties. Being part of a community of believers encourages us to remain steadfast. **Hebrews 10:24- 25** urges, "Let us consider how we may spur one another on toward love and good deeds, not giving up meeting together, as some are in the habit of doing, but encouraging one another." Godly friends and mentors can help us realign our priorities when we stray.

Practical Tip: Join a small group, Bible study, or church ministry. Share your struggles and victories with others who can pray for and encourage you.

Commit to Prayerful Surrender

Surrendering our divided loyalties to God requires humility and trust. **Proverbs 3:5-6** instructs us, "Trust in the Lord with all your heart and lean not on your own understanding; in all your ways submit to Him, and He will make your paths straight." We surrender our competing desires through prayer and ask God to guide our hearts.

Practical Tip: Begin each day with a prayer of surrender, asking God to direct your time, energy, and focus.

Real-Life Example: Navigating Competing Priorities

Michael, a successful businessman, struggled for years with balancing his work, family, and faith. Despite attending church weekly, he was consumed by his career, often working late and missing important family events. Over time, his spiritual life suffered, and he felt increasingly disconnected from God.

During a men's retreat, Michael was convicted by **Matthew 6:33:** "Seek first His kingdom and His righteousness, and all these things will be given to you as well." He realised that his divided loyalties prevented him from experiencing the fullness of God's presence.

Michael began implementing changes: he set boundaries on his work hours, committed to daily quiet time with God, and prioritised attending a small group. Though it required sacrifices, he found his life becoming more balanced, joyful, and purposeful. His relationships with his family and God flourished, and his career began to thrive in a healthier way.

Conclusion: Staying Focused on God

Overcoming divided loyalties is an ongoing journey that requires intentionality, self-awareness, and dependence on God. By prioritizing Him above all else, we discover the peace and fulfilment that come from a life aligned with His will. Remember the promise of James 4:8: "Come near to God and He will come near to you." As we draw closer to Him, He strengthens our hearts and helps us remain steadfast in our devotion.

When we prioritize God, everything else falls into its rightful place. Let us commit to a life of undivided loyalty, trusting that God's love and plans for us are far greater than anything the world can offer.

Chapter 13: Living in God's Presence

Cultivating a Lifestyle That Honours God in All Things

Living in God's presence is not confined to a single moment or place; it is a daily, continuous walk with Him. It involves intentionally aligning every aspect of your life—your thoughts, words, and actions—with His will. **Colossians 3:17** instructs, "And whatever you do, whether in word or deed, do it all in the name of the Lord Jesus, giving thanks to God the Father through Him." This verse captures the essence of a life lived in God's presence: honouring Him in all things and seeking His guidance in every decision.

In the Old Testament, God dwelled among His people in the Tabernacle, signifying His desire to be with them. However, through Jesus Christ, we now have the Holy Spirit dwelling within us, making God's presence accessible at all times. **1 Corinthians 6:19-20** reminds us, "Do you not know that your bodies are temples of the Holy Spirit, who is in you, whom you have received from God? You are not your own; you were bought at a price. Therefore honour God with your bodies." Cultivating a lifestyle that honours God involves recognising His nearness and letting it shape our daily choices.

Practical Ways to Live in God's Presence

Start the Day with God

The way you begin your day sets the tone for everything that follows. Spending time with God in prayer and Scripture at the start of your day centers your heart and mind on Him. **Psalm 5:3** says, "In the morning, Lord, you hear my voice; in the morning, I lay my requests before you and wait expectantly.

Practical Tip: Dedicate the first 15–30 minutes of your day to prayer and reading the Bible. Keep a journal to note down what God reveals to you during this time.

Practice Gratitude

Gratitude is a powerful way to live in God's presence. When we thank God for His blessings, we acknowledge His hand in every aspect of our lives. **1 Thessalonians 5:16-18** encourages us, "Rejoice always, pray continually, give thanks in all circumstances; for this is God's will for you in Christ Jesus."

Practical Tip: Keep a gratitude journal. Write down three things you are thankful for each evening, recognising God's presence in your day.

Invite God into Everyday Decisions

Living in God's presence means consulting Him in both major and minor decisions. **Proverbs 3:5-6** reminds us, "Trust in the Lord with all your heart and lean not on your own understanding; in all your ways submit to Him, and He will make your paths straight.

Practical Tip: Before making decisions whether at work, in relationships, or regarding finances pause and pray. Ask for God's wisdom and guidance.

Be Mindful of Your Thoughts and Words: Our thoughts and words reflect what is in our hearts. To honour God, we must be intentional about what we dwell on and speak. **Philippians 4:8** encourages us, "Whatever is true, whatever is noble, whatever is right, whatever is pure, whatever is lovely, whatever is admirable—if anything is excellent or praiseworthy—think about such things."

Practical Tip: Practice replacing negative thoughts with Scripture. For example, if you feel anxious, meditate on **Isaiah 41:10**, "Do not fear, for I am with you."

Serve Others with Love: Serving: others is a tangible way to reflect God's presence in your life. **Matthew 25:40** says, "Truly I tell you, whatever you did for one of the least of these brothers and sisters of mine, you did for me."

Practical Tip: Look for opportunities to serve, whether by volunteering, helping a neighbor, or offering encouragement to someone in need.

Cultivate an Awareness of God's Presence: A life in God's presence involves constant awareness of His nearness. This can be as simple as whispering prayers throughout the day or pausing to acknowledge His work in your life. **Acts 17:28** affirms, "For in Him we live and move and have our being."

Practical Tip: Set reminders on your phone to pause and thank God or to pray throughout the day. These moments can help refocus your heart on Him.

The Joy and Peace of Living in God's Presence Every Day

Living in God's presence brings profound joy and peace, regardless of life's circumstances. **Psalm 16:11** declares, "You make known to me the path of life; you will fill me with   joy in your presence, with eternal pleasures at your right hand." The more we dwell in God's presence, the more we experience His unchanging peace, even amid challenges.

Real-life Example: Sarah, a working mother of three, found herself overwhelmed by the demands of work, family, and ministry. She often felt distant from God and struggled to find peace. After attending a women's retreat, she was inspired to intentionally cultivate God's presence in her daily life. Sarah began starting her day with prayer, pausing during lunch breaks to meditate on Scripture, and ending her day with gratitude. Over time, she noticed a transformation. Herstress levels decreased, her relationships improved, and she felt a renewed closeness to God.

Conclusion: Embrace the Beauty of God's Presence

Living in God's presence is not about perfection but about devotion. It is a journey of drawing closer to Him daily, surrendering our lives to

His guidance, and experiencing the fullness of His love. **Isaiah 26:3** promises, "You will keep in perfect peace those whose minds are steadfast, because they trust in You."

When we intentionally cultivate a lifestyle that honours God, we discover the joy, peace, and fulfilment that come from living in harmony with His will. Let this chapter serve as a call to action: to seek God's presence in every moment and allow Him to transform every aspect of your life.

Chapter 14:
The Rewards of Devotion

The Blessings of Wholehearted Devotion to God

Wholehearted devotion to God is an act of obedience and a pathway to experiencing His blessings. God's Word assures us that when we seek Him with all our hearts, He rewards us abundantly. **Hebrews 11:6** declares, "And without faith, it is impossible to please God, because anyone who comes to Him must believe that He exists and that He rewards those who earnestly seek Him." When we place God at the centre of our lives, His promises unfold before us. These rewards often include peace that surpasses understanding, unshakable joy, divine guidance, and spiritual growth.

Biblical Examples of Devotion and Its Rewards

Abraham The Reward of Faithfulness Abraham is a prime example of someone who devoted himself entirely to God. His willingness to leave his home land and later to sacrifice Isaac demonstrated his unwavering trust in God. As a result, God blessed Abraham with descendants as numerous as the stars and made him the father of many nations **(Genesis 22:16-18)**.

Key Takeaway: Devotion to God often involves surrender and trust, even when the path is uncertain

God rewards such faith with His faithfulness and provision.

Hannah The Blessing of God's Favor In 1 Samuel 1, Hannah poured out her heart in prayer, devoting her deepest desires to God. She vowed to dedicate her son to the Lord if He granted her a child. God answered her prayers, giving her Samuel, who became one of Israel's greatest prophets.

Key Takeaway: When we devote our desires and burdens to God, He answers and uses our devotion to fulfil His greater purposes.

Paul The Joy of Eternal Perspective Despite enduring persecution, imprisonment, and hardships, Paul remained devoted to Christ. His reward was an unshakable joy and the assurance of eternal life. In 2 **Timothy 4:7-8**, Paul writes, "I have fought the good fight, I have finished the race, I have kept the faith. Now there is in store for me the crown of righteousness."

Key Takeaway: Wholehearted devotion may not always bring immediate earthly rewards, but it guarantees eternal blessings and a legacy of faith.

Personal Testimonies of Devotion's Rewards

Lisa's Story Peace in the Storm Lisa, a single mother of two, faced financial struggles that left her overwhelmed. In her desperation, she chose to devote herself to God, spending time daily in prayer and reading the Bible. Over time, she experienced peace, clarity in decision-making, and unexpected financial provision.

Reflection: Lisa's story shows how devotion to God can transform our perspective, allowing us to experience peace even in life's storms.

Mark's Story Purpose and Fulfilment: Mark, a successful businessman, felt an emptiness despite his accomplishments. He began attending a men's Bible study, where he rededicated his life to Christ. By devoting his business to God's principles,

Mark found renewed purpose and fulfilment in serving others through his work.

Reflection: Devotion to God reshapes our ambitions, leading to a life of purpose and impact.

The Blessings of Devotion in Modern Life

In a world filled with anxiety, devotion to God provides peace. Jesus promises in **Matthew 11:28- 29**, "Come to me, all you who are weary and burdened, and I will give you rest." Those who devote themselves to God experience rest for their souls, free from the chaos of worldly distractions.

Wisdom and Guidance: Devotion brings clarity. **Proverbs 3:5-6** reminds us, "Trust in the Lord with all your heart and lean not on your own understanding; in all your ways submit to Him, and He will make your paths straight."

Joy and Contentment: Devotion shifts our focus from temporary pleasures to eternal treasures. **Psalm 37:4** says, "Take delight in the Lord, and He will give you the desires of your heart." This joy transcends circumstances and brings lasting fulfilment.

Strength and Resilience: Those devoted to God find strength to endure trials. **Isaiah 40:31** declares, "But those who hope in the Lord will renew their strength." Devotion builds spiritual resilience, enabling us to persevere through life's challenges.

Practical Steps to Deepen Devotion and Experience Its Rewards

Commit to Daily Time with God: Begin and end each day in prayer and Scripture. Make this a non-negotiable part of your routine.

Serve Others Selflessly: Find ways to use your time, talents, and resources to bless others. Service is an act of devotion that pleases God.

Align Your Goals with God's Will: Surrender your ambitions and seek God's purpose for your life. Trust that His plans are better than yours (Jeremiah 29:11).

Stay Connected to a Faith Community: Surround yourself with fellow believers who encourage and challenge you in your devotion to God.

Conclusion:
The Joy of Wholehearted Devotion

The rewards of devotion to God are immeasurable. They extend beyond material blessings to include peace, joy, purpose, and the assurance of His presence. In **Psalm 84:11**, we are reminded, "For the Lord God is a sun and shield; the Lord bestows favor and honour; no good thing does He withhold from those whose walk is blameless."

As you continue to live a life of devotion, celebrate the depth of God's love and the abundant blessings He pours into the lives of those who seek Him. Let this chapter inspire you to remain steadfast in your commitment, knowing that the rewards of devotion are eternal and deeply fulfiling.

The next Chapter brings the book to a powerful close by summarizing the key lessons about God's jealous love and the transformation it brings when we embrace a life of exclusive worship and devotion. Chapter 15 serves as a final call to action, encouraging readers to commit wholeheartedly to God and experience the joy of living in alignment with His divine purpose.

Chapter 15:
A Life Fully Devoted to God

Embracing the Call to Exclusive Worship

Throughout this journey, we have explored the depths of God's jealous love and its call for our exclusive worship. From understanding the nature of His jealousy to recognising the idols that compete for our devotion, we have seen how God longs for a relationship with us that is wholehearted, faithful, and transformational.

Exodus 34:14 reminds us: "Do not worship any other god, for the Lord, whose name is Jealous, is a jealous God." This jealousy is not rooted in insecurity but in God's perfect love—a love that desires the best for us and grieves when we settle for anything less than Him.

When we embrace the call to exclusive worship, we open our hearts to the life-changing power of His presence. The distractions, idols, and divided loyalties of this world lose their hold as we experience the peace, joy, and purpose that come from living fully devoted to God.

The Transformation of a Devoted Life

Freedom from Idolatry Exclusive worship frees us from the burdens of chasing temporary pleasures or relying on things that ultimately cannot satisfy. Jesus said in **Matthew 6:24**, "No one can serve two masters." When we choose God, we find true freedom.

Intimacy with God Devotion deepens our relationship with the Creator. As we draw near to Him through prayer, worship, and His Word, we experience His nearness and His guidance. **James 4:8** encourages, "Draw near to God, and He will draw near to you."

Transformation of Character A life devoted to God transforms us into His likeness. The Holy Spirit works within us to produce the fruit of the Spirit: love, joy, peace, patience, kindness, goodness, faithfulness, gentleness, and self-control (Galatians 5:22-23).

Eternal Perspective

Living for God aligns our priorities with eternity. The fleeting concerns of this world fade as we focus on His kingdom and His righteousness.

A Final Invitation to Surrender

God's jealous love invites us into a challenging and rewarding relationship. It requires surrender—letting go of our need for control and trusting Him with every aspect of our lives.

Romans 12:1 urges us: "Therefore, I urge you, brothers and sisters, in view of God's mercy, to offer your bodies as a living sacrifice, holy and pleasing to God—this is your true and proper worship." This act of surrender is not a loss but a gain—a step into the fullness of life God desires for us.

Practical Steps to Fully Surrender

Daily Commitment Begin each day with a prayer of surrender, inviting God to guide your thoughts, decisions, and actions.

Examine Your Heart Regularly assess your priorities. Are there areas where you struggle to give God first place?

Trust God's Plan Trusting God's will often means relinquishing your own. Reflect on **Proverbs 3:5-6**: "Trust in the Lord with all your heart and lean not on your own understanding; in all your ways submit to Him, and He will make your paths straight."

Live with Gratitude A grateful heart recognizes God's blessings and responds with devotion. Cultivate a habit of thanking Him daily.

Celebrating God's Jealous Love

God's jealousy is not a burden but a blessing. It reveals His deep commitment to us and His desire for our ultimate good. As we respond to His call, we are transformed into people who reflect His glory, love His ways, and trust His plans.

2 Chronicles 16:9 declares, "For the eyes of the Lord range throughout the earth to strengthen those whose hearts are fully committed to Him." Let this promise inspire you to live with unwavering devotion, knowing God's strength, love, and blessings are with you.

A Life Fully Devoted to God

As we conclude, let this be a moment of decision. Will you embrace the call to exclusive worship? Will you surrender fully to the jealous love of the God who created you, redeems you, and desires an intimate relationship with you?

Living a life fully devoted to God is not about perfection but persistence—a daily choice to seek Him first, trust Him completely, and love Him wholeheartedly.

May you walk in the beauty of His jealous love, experiencing the joy, peace, and purpose that come from a life fully surrendered to Him. This is the reward of devotion—a life transformed by the One who loves you with an everlasting love.

Chapter 16: Reflection and Prayer

A Time for Personal Reflection

As we close this journey into the beauty of God's jealous love, take a moment to pause and reflect on what you have learned. Throughout these chapters, God's unwavering desire for a close relationship with you has been revealed. His call to exclusive worship, surrender, and devotion is an invitation to experience the fullness of life in Him.

Consider the following questions to guide your reflection

Where is my heart? What or who holds the greatest priority in my life? Is God truly first in my heart and decisions?

What idols do I need to release? Are distractions, habits, or desires competing with my devotion to God?

How am I cultivating intimacy with God? Am I spending consistent time in prayer, worship, and Scripture? What changes can I make to deepen my relationship with Him?

What steps can I take to surrender more fully? Are there areas in my life where I struggle to trust God's plan? How can I let go and trust His will completely?

Take time to write your thoughts, prayers, and commitments. Allow this to be a sacred moment of honest conversation with God.

Shola Ajibade

A Closing Prayer

Let this prayer serve as a guide for surrender and devotion

Heavenly Father,

I come before You with a heart longing to know You more deeply. Thank You for loving me with a jealous love—a love so strong that it pursues me and calls me to a life of fullness in You. Lord, I confess that there have been times when I have allowed other things to take priority over You. I ask for Your forgiveness and grace to return my heart to You. Help me to release every idol, every distraction, and every fear that keeps me from living in wholehearted devotion to You.

Teach me to walk in Your ways, to trust Your plans, and to find my joy in Your presence. May my life reflect Your holiness and love as I seek to honour You in all things. Strengthen me when I struggle and remind me that Your grace is sufficient.

Lord, I surrender my heart, my mind, my soul, and my strength to You. Be my first love, my greatest treasure, and my eternal hope. I choose today and every day to live for You alone.

In Jesus' name, I pray.

Amen.

Final Encouragement

As you move forward, remember that God's jealous love is a life long journey, not a one-time event. It requires daily surrender, but it also comes with daily grace.

You are not alone. God walks with you, strengthens you, and empowers you to live a life fully devoted to Him. Trust in His promises, lean into His presence, and celebrate the joy of belonging to a God who loves you fiercely and unconditionally.

May your life be a testament to the power of exclusive worship and the beauty of God's jealous love.

Glossary

Jealousy (God's) – In the context of **Exodus 34:14**, God's jealousy refers to His intense desire for exclusive devotion and worship from His people. Unlike human jealousy, which stems from insecurity or selfishness, God's jealousy is pure, righteous, and protective, as He longs to safeguard His relationship with His creation.

Covenant – A binding agreement or promise. In the Bible, God establishes covenants with His people, pledging His love, faithfulness, and protection in exchange for their devotion and obedience.

Idolatry – The worship of idols or false gods, or the act of placing anything—other than God—at the center of one's heart, devotion, and worship. Idolatry is considered a sin in Scripture because it undermines the exclusive worship due to God alone.

Exclusive Worship – The practice of devoting all of one's heart, mind, and soul to the worship of God alone, rejecting all other forms of worship or distractions that would take precedence over God.

Spiritual Infidelity – The act of turning away from God and breaking the covenant relationship with Him, often through idolatry or disobedience. It is likened to betrayal in a marriage relationship.

Holiness – The state of being set apart for God's purposes. God's holiness means He is pure, righteous, and without sin, deserving of total reverence and worship.

Repentance – A heartfelt turning away from sin and returning to God with a desire to change one's life and align with His will. Repentance is an essential part of maintaining a right relationship with God.

Devotion – A deep, committed love and dedication to God, expressed through worship, obedience, and prioritizing His presence in one's life.

Sacredness – The quality of being holy, deserving of reverence and honour. Sacredness is often applied to God, His name, and things related to Him, such as the Bible and worship.

Redemption – The act of God saving His people from sin and its consequences, restoring them to a right relationship with Him. In the Bible, this is ultimately fulfiled through the death and resurrection of Jesus Christ.

Intimacy with God – A close, personal relationship with God that goes beyond ritual and religious practice. It involves a deep connection, trust, and constant communion with Him through prayer, worship, and obedience.

Grace – Unmerited favor from God, given freely to humanity, allowing for forgiveness, salvation, and a restored relationship with Him. It is by grace that believers are empowered to live in accordance with God's will.

Worship – The act of showing reverence and honour to God. Worship can take many forms, such as prayer, song, praise, or living a life that reflects God's love and truth.

Faithfulness – Remaining true, loyal, and steadfast to a relationship or commitment. God is described as faithful to His promises, and He calls His people to be faithful in their relationship with Him.

Obedience – The act of following God's commandments and living according to His will. Obedience is a key component of the covenant relationship with God and is tied to the idea of loyalty and worship.

Spiritual Warfare – The ongoing struggle between the forces of good (God) and evil (Satan) in the lives of believers. Spiritual warfare often involves resisting temptation, idolatry, and anything that would draw people away from God's truth.

Surrender – The act of yielding to God's authority and control, allowing Him to guide one's life. Surrender is an essential step in growing in faith and devotion to God.

Grace vs. Law – The distinction between living under God's grace, which offers salvation through faith in Jesus Christ, and the law, which refers to the commandments and rules in the Old Testament. Christians are called to live by grace, not by the law, though the law still reveals God's holiness and standards.

Fellowship with God – A close, intimate relationship and partnership with God, characterized by communication (prayer), mutual love, and shared purpose.

Holy Spirit – The third person of the Trinity, the Holy Spirit empowers believers to live godly lives, convicts of sin, and helps in the process of sanctification. This glossary provides definitions of key terms to help better understand the concepts discussed in the book and in their personal journey of faith.

References

The Holy Bible, New International Version. Zondervan, 2011.

Adams, J. (2009). The Heart of Worship: The Call to Give God Our Best. Faith Publishing.

Carson, D. A. (2008). *The Gagging of God: Christianity Confronts Pl

Bible References

Exodus 34:14

"For you shall worship no other god, for the Lord, whose name is Jealous, is a jealous God." God's call for exclusive worship and His intense desire for the devotion of His people.

Deuteronomy 4:24

"For the Lord your God is a consuming fire, a jealous God."

Reinforces God's holiness and the intensity of His jealousy for His people's undivided worship.

James 4:5

"Or do you think Scripture says without reason that he jealously longs for the spirit he has caused to dwell in us?"

Emphasises that God desires our whole hearts, and His jealousy is a sign of His intense love and longing for a relationship with us.

Exodus 20:3-5

"You shall have no other gods before me. You shall not make for yourselves a carved image... for I, the Lord your God, am a jealous God..."

The first commandment establishes the foundation for exclusive worship and highlights God's intolerance of idolatry.

Matthew 22:37

"Love the Lord your God with all your heart and with all your soul and with all your mind."

Jesus' teaching on the greatest commandment, which calls for total devotion to God, aligning with His desire for exclusive worship.

1 John 5:21

"Dear children, keep yourselves from idols."

Jealous For You

A call in the New Testament to avoid idolatry, reinforcing the importance of keeping God at the center of our worship.

2 Corinthians 11:2

"I am jealous for you with a godly jealousy. I promised you to one husband, to Christ, so that I might present you as a pure virgin to him."

Paul's letter to the Corinthians, expressing godly jealousy for their purity and devotion to Christ.

Isaiah 42:8

"I am the Lord, that is my name! I will not yield my glory to another or my praise to idols."

A declaration of God's desire for His exclusive glory and worship.

Romans 12:1-2

"Therefore, I urge you, brothers and sisters, in view of God's mercy, to offer your bodies as a living sacrifice, holy and pleasing to God—this is your true and proper worship. Do not conform to the pattern of this world, but be transformed by the renewing of your mind."

A call for believers to offer their lives as living sacrifices, rejecting worldly idols and devoting themselves fully to God.

Hosea 2:19-20

"I will betroth you to me forever; I will betroth you in righteousness and justice, love and compassion. I will betroth you in faithfulness, and you will acknowledge the Lord."

A beautiful metaphor of God's covenantal love for His people, calling them to exclusive devotion.

Psalm 115:4-8

"But their idols are silver and gold, made by human hands. They have mouths, but cannot speak, eyes, but cannot see..."

A passage warning against the futility of idol worship and the emptiness of anything that competes with God for worship.

Matthew 6:24

"No one can serve two masters. Either you will hate the one and love the other, or you will be devoted to the one and despise the other."

Jesus teaches that devotion to God cannot coexist with devotion to other idols or false gods.

Jeremiah 2:13

"My people have committed two sins: they have forsaken me, the spring of living water, and have dug their own cisterns, broken cisterns that cannot hold water."

God condemns idolatry, where people turn to other sources for fulfilment, instead of trusting in Him.

Philippians 3:18-19

"For, as I have often told you before and now tell you again, even with tears, many live as enemies of the cross of Christ.

Their destiny is destruction, their god is their stomach, and their glory is in their shame."

A warning against making earthly pleasures or desires idols, which can draw us away from God's true purpose.

Revelation 21:3-4

"And I heard a loud voice from the throne saying, 'Look! God's dwelling place is now among the people, and he will dwell with them. They will be his people, and God himself will be with them and be their God.'"

A vision of the ultimate fulfilment of God's desire for a relationship with His people, where there is no more idol or distraction, only His presence.

These Bible references offer deeper insights into God's call for exclusive worship, His jealousy for His people, and the importance of keeping Him at the centre of our lives. Each reference emphasizes

Jealous For You

God's passionate desire for undivided devotion and warns against the dangers of idolatry.

Author's Note

Dear Reader,

Thank you for picking up this book, 'Jealous for You.' I share these words with you with great joy and deep gratitude. Throughout my journey of faith, I have understood the profound meaning behind God's desire. Someday, I will share my personal journey with God. I made terrible mistakes that cost me so much pain, anguish and anxiety. But God came through, just by putting Him in the Centre of all I do. He wiped my tears and brought me out of the slimy pit - Psalm 40:2, which states: *"He lifted me out of the slimy pit, out of the mud and mire; he set my feet on a rock and gave me a firm place to stand."* That is what He can do when we make Him the Centre of everything we do and exclusively worship Him.

For exclusive worship, as expressed in Exodus 34:14. His jealousy is not born from insecurity or possessiveness, but from a perfect love that longs for us to experience the fullness of His presence.

In a world filled with distractions and competing desires, it's easy to let other things take the place of God in our hearts. But through this book, I hope to guide you toward recognising those idols in your life, and, ultimately, to rediscover the incredible peace, purpose, and fulfilment that come from a life centered on Him.

As you read, I encourage you to reflect deeply on your own relationship with God. May this journey lead you to a deeper understanding of His love and a renewed commitment to worshiping Him with all of your heart, soul, and mind.

Thank you for allowing me to be part of your faith journey. I pray that you are blessed, transformed, and drawn closer to God through these pages.

With heartfelt
blessings,

Shola Ajibade

www.ingramcontent.com/pod-product-compliance
Lightning Source LLC
Chambersburg PA
CBHW052113070526
44584CB00017B/2462